Cobi Jones Soccer Games

By Cobi Jones
and Andrew Gutelle

Illustrated by
Paul Meisel

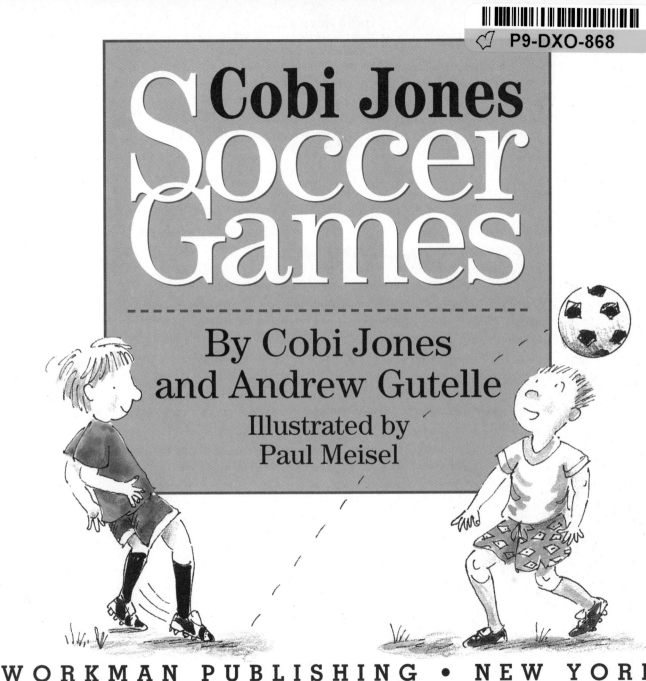

WORKMAN PUBLISHING • NEW YORK

PHOTO CREDITS

Cover, box, and pages 1, 8, 23, 25, 35, 38, 48, 59, 66, 68, 70, 72, 85, 97 copyright © Tom Di Pace
Pages 9, 73: Stephen Dunn/ALLSPORT
Pages 26, 67: Duomo
Page 13: Essy G./MLS/ALLSPORT
Page 31: Rick Rickman/Duomo
Pages 3, 15, 74: William R. Sallaz/Duomo
Pages 12, 45, 84, 96: Jamie Squire/ALLSPORT
Page 58: Chris Trotman/Duomo
Back Cover: Tom Di Pace

Library of Congress Cataloging-in-Publication Data
Jones, Cobi.
Cobi Jones soccer games /by Cobi Jones and Andrew Gutelle; illustrated by Paul Meisel.
p. cm.
Summary: Promotes the development of the fundamental skills of soccer through thirty games, drills, exercises,
sets of instruction, and professional tips. Includes a size 4 practice soccer ball.
ISBN 0-7611-1270-7 (pbk.)
1. Soccer—Juvenile literature. [1. Soccer] I. Gutelle, Andrew. II. Meisel, Paul, ill. III. Title.
GV943.25.J65 1998   98—24660
796.334—dc21   CIP
                             AC

Workman books are available at special discounts when purchased in bulk for premiums and
sales promotions as well as for fund-raising or educational use. Special editions can also be
created to specification. For details, contact the
Special Sales Director at the address below.

Workman Publishing Company, Inc.
708 Broadway
New York, NY 10003-9555
http://www.workmanweb.com

Printed in United States of America

First printing October 1998

10 9 8 7 6 5 4 3 2

Acknowledgments

Thanks to Ashley Michael Hammond, Glen Pernia, and the crew at Ashley's Soccer Camp, Inc., in Montclair, New Jersey, for their good advice and spirited play. Also thanks to John Salvatore of *Soccer Extreme* in Waterbury, Connecticut, for his helpful suggestions.

This book would not have been possible without the assistance of Peter Workman, Paul Hanson, Paul Gamarello, and the entire Workman Publishing team. A special thanks to our editor, Anne Kostick, who guided us from the opening kickoff through sudden-death overtime, and into print.

Contents

Kicking

Dribbling

Passing

Trapping

Juggling

About Cobi Jones

Cobi Jones, one of the most exciting and popular soccer players in the country, has twice played World Cup on the U.S. National Team. Cobi was born in Detroit, Michigan, but grew up playing soccer in Southern California. After starring at West Lake High School, he tried out for the UCLA college team. Cobi made the squad and eventually became an All-American. When he is not playing for the national team, Cobi is a Major League Soccer (MLS) all-star midfielder for Los Angeles Galaxy.

THE COBI JONES PRACTICE BALL

This package includes your specially printed (size 4) soccer ball and a plastic inflation pin.

HOW TO INFLATE:

1. Attach the inflation pin to a small pump like the kind used to fill bicycle tires with air.

2. Moisten the pin and gently insert it into the airhole on the ball. Pump! The ball is fully inflated when it feels firm when you squeeze it.

3. Remove the pin from the ball and store it in a safe place. You may need to add a little air to your ball from time to time.

HOW TO USE THE PRACTICE BALL:

1. Place your ball with the sun design pointing straight up toward the sky (sun=sun).

2. To keep the ball moving close to the ground, aim your foot and kick directly at the band around the center of the ball.

3. To make the ball rise into the air, kick just below the band.

4. To learn some basic kicks, see the instructions on pages 18 and 40.

Getting Started

Imagine the perfect sport. It should be easy so that kids can play, yet challenging enough to test the skills of a world-class athlete. It would definitely not need a lot of fancy or expensive equipment—maybe just a ball to get things rolling and some room to run. The rules would be so simple that even a kindergarten kid could understand them. And finally, the game would have to be a whole lot of fun. You've just imagined soccer—the most popular sport on the planet.

Soccer is played by people of all ages in every corner of the world. And now you're ready to join them. In this book you will find games and activities designed for kids who want to have a good time while learning to play soccer.

Best of all, you will meet Cobi Jones, who plays for the United States World Cup team and pro soccer's Los Angeles Galaxy. Cobi has lots of tips and ideas that can help make you the best player possible.

"I started playing when I was five years old. My cousin is only a year older than I am, and I always liked to do whatever he was doing. One day when my parents and I were driving in the car, I saw him out there playing soccer. I asked my parents if I could play too. They stopped the car and talked to the coach. He tossed me a uniform, and I joined the team. I've been playing ever since."

RATING THE GAMES

Most of the games in this book are so easy that anyone can try them. A few need a little extra time to learn or skill to play. Here is a guide to help you find the games that are best for you.

 This means a game is especially good for beginners. Start with these if you are playing for the first time.

 These games take a little bit of skill. Don't be afraid to try them, even if you are still learning the soccer basics.

 These games are for more experienced players. Try them when you and your friends are ready for more of a challenge.

SOCCER GEAR

Both of these kids are dressed to play soccer. One of them is going to kick a ball in the backyard, while the other is going to play in an organized game.

Water bottle: If you go all-out on a hot day, you'll need it!

Uniform: Shorts and shirt of a lightweight material keep you cool when the action heats up.

Lightweight clothes: Soccer players are always on the go, so don't overdress.

Scrimmage vests: For practicing when you join a team.

Shin guards: They protect your legs from accidental kicks.

Sneakers: Choose a pair that supports your ankles and lets you run fast.

Soccer socks: They fold down to cover your shin guards.

Soccer shoes: Studs on the bottom help you make quick twists and turns.

SOCCER RULES

Y ou have probably been kicking balls since you could walk, but you may be new to soccer. In that case, here are the official rules:

Soccer is a contest between two teams, with 11 players on each side. The game is played on a large rectangular field. A pro soccer field is usually wider and longer than a football field. At each end is a goal. The object of the game is to—what else?—score goals. To do this, a player must shoot the ball into the other team's goal. The goalkeeper is the only player who is allowed to touch the ball with his hands. Other players must use their feet to move the ball. They can also use their heads, chests, thighs—anything but their hands and arms.

Soccer is an action game. As long as the ball is on the field and there are no in-juries or fouls, the game keeps going. When one team kicks the ball off the field, the other puts it back into play. They may throw it or kick it, depending on the situation.

A professional game is 90 minutes long. At the end of a game, the team that has scored the most goals wins.

YOUTH SOCCER

If you are already playing on a soccer team, you may notice that the rules used in your games are a bit different. Young players start out on smaller fields. They play a shorter game, broken into two halves or even four quarters. There are often fewer than 11 players on a side. Many youth soccer leagues play seven against seven. But one thing that never changes is the object of the game—kick that ball and score goals!

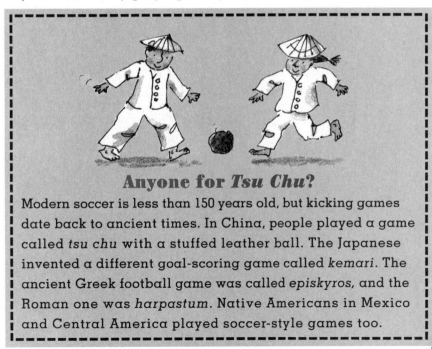

Anyone for *Tsu Chu*?

Modern soccer is less than 150 years old, but kicking games date back to ancient times. In China, people played a game called *tsu chu* with a stuffed leather ball. The Japanese invented a different goal-scoring game called *kemari*. The ancient Greek football game was called *episkyros*, and the Roman one was *harpastum*. Native Americans in Mexico and Central America played soccer-style games too.

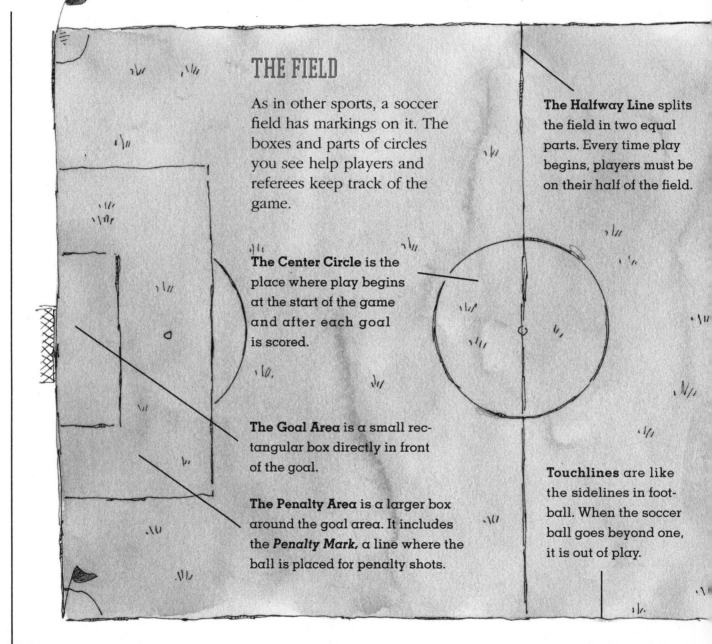

THE FIELD

As in other sports, a soccer field has markings on it. The boxes and parts of circles you see help players and referees keep track of the game.

The Center Circle is the place where play begins at the start of the game and after each goal is scored.

The Goal Area is a small rectangular box directly in front of the goal.

The Penalty Area is a larger box around the goal area. It includes the *Penalty Mark,* a line where the ball is placed for penalty shots.

The Halfway Line splits the field in two equal parts. Every time play begins, players must be on their half of the field.

Touchlines are like the sidelines in football. When the soccer ball goes beyond one, it is out of play.

MARK YOUR OWN SOCCER FIELD

Between my hat and my backpack and as high as my head is your goal!

One of the best things about soccer is that you can play it anywhere—in parks, schoolyards, or even backyards. Here are some things to remember when setting up your field:

Always start with goals. Use coats, hats, or extra soccer balls to identify the "goalposts." Avoid using rocks or anything else that might hurt a player who falls on one. Pace off the two goals carefully to make sure they are the same size.

The distance from one goal to the other will define the field. Think about the number of players on each side. Make the field large, but not so big that the players will be exhausted from running across it.

Don't worry about penalty areas, the center circle, or other official lines. You can estimate where they are if you need them or add them in future games.

Finally, go over the ground rules. Is any ball between the goalposts a score? (In soccer, the crossbar is eight feet high.) Can players range as far as they want to the sides? Make the rules fit your field and your skill level.

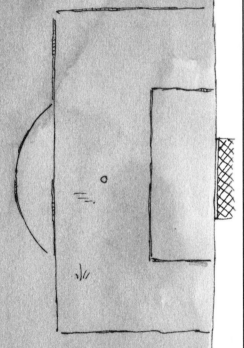

Goal Lines mark the ends of the field. A ball that goes over the line to either side of the goal is out of play.

Corner Flags mark small spaces at the four corners of the field. Players take corner kicks from these spots.

"**M**y friends and I never needed a lot of space when we wanted to play. At my friend's house, the goal was always between the mailbox and the tree. If there were a lot of us and we couldn't find a field to play on, we would play on the blacktop. I remember falling down, getting scrapes and bruises and thinking nothing of it."

WHO'S WHO?

This particular youth soccer team plays in a league with seven players on a side.

Teams can set up their players in different ways. This one is playing a 2-2-2 lineup in front of its goalie.

Forwards play up where they can score goals. Forwards who play along the sides of the fields are often called *wings*.

Midfielders patrol the center of the field. They are often called *halfbacks*.

Remember that the setup you see here is just one example. A team can strengthen its defense by using two fullbacks plus a third defender called a *sweeper*. To control the middle of the field, it may use a center midfielder between its two halfbacks. For maximum offense, it may use a third goal-scoring forward called a *striker*. It all depends on the players and on their coach's plan for the game.

"Defenders are usually some of the bigger players because they have to stop crosses and battle forwards near the goal. Midfielders often have extremely good endurance because they need to run up and down and play a lot of offense and defense. They need to be good passers and work well under pressure. Forwards must be calm under pressure and very precise. They get only so many opportunities to score, so they need to be very accurate."

Defenders play closest to the goalie. They are often called *fullbacks*.

The **Goalkeeper** patrols the penalty area. He may touch the ball with his hands as long as he is in the penalty area.

WARMING UP

Soccer players need to be ready to run. And stop, start, jump, twist, slide, kick, leap, bend, and stretch. You never know which of your muscles you will need at any moment, so be sure to warm up before you begin to play. Dribbling your soccer ball is one great way to loosen up. You can also try some of these simple warm-up exercises and games.

CRISSCROSS

Start with a simple exercise that stretches your leg muscles. Cross your legs so that the outsides of your feet are together. Bend from the waist and try to touch your toes several times. Stretch slowly, and be sure not to bounce up and down. Now cross your legs with the other one in front and touch your toes again.

TOE TAP

This warm-up can be done by yourself, even though you are using a ball. Place your soccer ball on the ground in front of you. Now tap the top of the ball with one foot, then switch feet and tap the top with the other. Keep switching feet for 25 taps in a row. If you are not out of breath, try adding another 25 taps. See if you can pick up the pace and do your taps faster.

STRETCH UP

Now stretch out some other leg muscles. Stand with your two feet in a line; there should be about a foot of space between your front heel and your back toe. Lean forward slowly, bending your front knee. Feel the stretch in your leg. Hold that position for a few seconds and then relax. After several stretches, switch so the foot that was behind is now in front and try again.

FIND THE LEADER

In this simple warm-up exercise, players stand in a circle. One person is the leader. Holding the soccer ball with both hands she tap, tap, taps it on her leg.

Then she moves to her chest, head, or wherever she wants with steady taps. Everyone else in the circle has a ball too. Each person follows the leader. Once there is a good rhythm going, the leader picks up the pace, tapping faster and faster as the others follow along.

You can easily turn this into a game. One player hides his eyes so that he does not know who the leader is. Can he figure out the leader by watching the tappers? Take turns leading and being the player who guesses.

ONE-LEGGED CATCH

Since one leg is often kicking the ball, soccer players must frequently balance on the other one. When you warm up, stand on one leg facing a friend. Toss the ball back and forth but try not to lose your balance. Now switch and practice standing on your other leg.

CHOOSING SIDES

Many soccer-style games need two teams. Here are some ways to think about setting up teams for the games in this book:

GET IN LINE: This is one of the simplest and fairest ways to get started. Once you form a line, pick every other player to make a team. You can try lining up from shortest to tallest or in alphabetical order.

PICK PAPERS: Write each person's name on a piece of paper and put them in a bag. Pick out half the names to form a team.

PICK CAPTAINS: Two players can be in charge of putting together teams. To be fair, they should be players of equal skill. They do not have to be the two best players.

WHO'S IT?

Many of the games you are about to play need one player to be IT or to go first. Here are 10 ways you might try choosing that person.

CHOOSE . . .

1. The oldest player
2. The youngest player
3. The person whose birthday is next
4. The person who brought the soccer ball
5. The person who can name the most state capitals
6. The person who can balance a soccer ball on his head longest
7. The person who can stand on one foot longest
8. The person with the longest last name
9. The person who won the last game must be IT the next time
10. The person who lost the last game gets to go first this time

Cobi's SOCCER Tips

1. Play with your soccer ball as much as you can. The best thing when you start out is to touch the ball as often as you possibly can.

2. Don't be afraid to try different skills when you are very young. It doesn't matter how well you can do them as long as you try.

3. Be a confident person. Don't let others discourage you. If you want to do something and you think you can do it, go for it!

Kicking

As soon as you drop a soccer ball onto a field, you're ready to start playing. After all, you already have the most important piece of soccer equipment you will ever need—your feet!

"When I was a kid, I used to kick my soccer ball around the house—through the house, up the stairs, all over the place. I used to kick it nonstop against the stairs. I tried to hit every step in a row going up and every step coming back down. My parents would tell me to stop and I would, but then an hour later I would start kicking it again. I just loved playing."

A soccer player quickly learns to kick in different ways. During a game he may need to send quick, accurate passes or long, looping ones. He might rocket a scoring shot into the goal or slip the ball between the goalie's legs. These moves and many others are possible because of the many ways you can kick a soccer ball. However, before you try any fancy footwork you need to work on the basics.

MEET YOUR FEET

Soccer players know how to get the most out of their feet. They have learned that during a game just about every part of your foot comes in handy:

Instep: The spot on your foot that gives kicks maximum power.

Sides: Use the inside and the outside for short passes.

Ankle: Locking it in place adds distance and accuracy to many shots and passes.

Toes: Pointing them down helps control the direction of your kicks.

Sole: You can use the bottom of your foot to stop a rolling soccer ball and get it under control.

Heel: For passes to teammates on the field behind you.

Before you start kicking, you need to get a feel for your soccer ball. Sit or kneel

This instep practice can help strengthen your feet for passing.

on the ground with your foot in front of you. Tap the ball on the top of your foot, just above your big toe. This spot, called your instep, is the place where your foot will often hit the ball.

Now put the ball on the ground. Have someone hold the ball in place with his foot. Kick it gently so that your instep hits just below the middle of the ball. Feel the ball and foot coming together. Try to kick a little harder so that you will know what to expect when your foot meets the ball in a real game.

"Whenever you kick, first look at the target you are trying to hit, then look at the ball. Once you look at the target, your brain will remember where the ball is supposed to go. From then on, keep your eye on the ball.

You want to hit the ball right about in the middle to get a good strike on it."

Kickoff

RATING: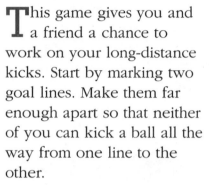

This game gives you and a friend a chance to work on your long-distance kicks. Start by marking two goal lines. Make them far enough apart so that neither of you can kick a ball all the way from one line to the other.

Players place their soccer balls on opposite goal lines. Running up to your ball, use your instep kick to blast it toward the other goal line. At the same time, your friend kicks his soccer ball, which rolls toward you.

When your friend's ball rolls to a stop, kick it back toward him. He will do the same thing with your soccer ball. Keep kicking until one of you makes a shot that rolls over the goal. When it does, that kicker has won the round.

You might want to add another rule so that the game uses more soccer skills. Instead of letting the ball roll to a stop, you may run over and stop it with your foot. By getting to a ball and stopping it quickly, you can improve your field position. That gives you a better chance to score with your next kick.

Hide and Kick

RATING:

This game is based on an old street game called Kick the Can. Long, strong kicks are one part of it. Play in a park or some other place with open space *and* lots of good hiding places.

To begin, mark a home base and set your soccer ball in the middle of it. One player runs up and kicks the ball with all her might. As she does, she shouts the name of another player, who immediately becomes IT. He runs after the soccer ball, and when he reaches it, he shuts his eyes and counts out loud to 50. (The other players have already taken off for hiding places, but counting gives them added time to disappear.)

Now IT kicks the ball back to home base. He leaves it there and begins his search for the hiding players. When he spots someone he races back to home base, kicks the ball, and shouts his name.

If IT wanders too far from the ball, hiding players can dash home and kick the ball first. Then all the players must race home before IT retrieves the ball.

Play as many times as you want. The player who is IT in one round gets to make the kick and choose the person who will be IT in the next one.

17

THE INSTEP KICK

The instep kick is one of the most important kicks you need to learn. Use it any time you want to kick the ball far. It is probably the best way to make a long pass down the field or to power the ball past the goalie.

To make the ball go straight, you must approach it from a slight angle.

ON YOUR MARK!

● Place the ball a few feet in front of you. You want to be able to run forward as you kick.

● Pick a spot down the field where you want to send the ball. With your head down, focus your eyes on the ball.

GET SET!

● Approach the ball from a slight angle. Take a few quick steps forward, and plant your non-kicking, or "plant foot," a few inches to the side of the ball. Your knee should be bent slightly and your plant foot should point in the direction you want the ball to go.

● As that foot lands, lean backward just a bit. Bring your shooting leg back as much as you can and bend it at the knee.

KICK!

● Swing your leg forward. As your knee passes over the ball, straighten your leg and kick.

● Strike the middle of the ball with your instep. Keep your toes pointed and your ankle locked.

As you follow through, your leg should keep going in the direction that you just kicked the ball. Remember to keep looking at the ball and to get your whole body into the kick.

As soon as you finish, get in position to make another play. The action never stops in soccer and neither should you!

Put A-SOCK in It!
The rest of the world calls it *football*, but in the United States it's soccer. The name comes from the early days in England when it was called "Association Football" or "Assoc" (A-SOCK) for short. For some reason, the name traveled across the Atlantic Ocean and stuck.

Touchdown

RATING:

This team game mixes soccer kicking with football scoring. You need only one soccer ball, and any number of kids can play.

Begin by marking the sides of a soccer goal. For starters, make the goal about 10 steps wide. Now add your kicking zones. Take five giant steps out from the goal and mark that spot with a hat or towel. That will be the field goal spot. Take another 15 steps and mark that spot for touchdowns.

The first player decides whether to go for a field goal or touchdown. He places the ball down at that spot and with one kick tries to put it in the goal. If he scores a field goal, his team gets 3 points. If he scores a touchdown, his team gets 6 points, plus he can go for the extra point. He takes an extra kick from the field goal marker and gets 1 point if that shot goes between the goalposts.

Take turns so that a player from one team follows a player from the other. As in football, the game is divided into quarters. Every player gets one chance per quarter, and the team that scores the most points wins.

5 v. 2

RATING:

Five Versus Two is a challenging all-around game for seven players. It provides offensive players a chance to work on kicking while defenders polish their skills.

Five players spread out evenly to form a circle. They stand at their spots kicking a ball to one another. Meanwhile the other two players —the defenders—set up in the circle. Working together but staying inside the circle, they try to take the ball away.

This is usually played as a one-touch game, which means you must kick the moving ball as it arrives. This may be too difficult when you are starting out, so try it as a two-touch game. A player can stop the ball with his foot (one touch) and then kick it (two touch). Another way to make it easier is to put one player in the middle and play 6 v. 1.

Don't be afraid to make other changes to fit your situation. If there are there eight kids who want to play, try a round of 6 v. 2. Only five kids today? Set up and play 4 v. 1. Experiment to see which combinations work best for you and your friends.

TRICKY KICKS

BANANA KICK

Like a curving baseball, this shot bends as it flies through the air. In certain situations a player may use the banana kick to curve the ball around a wall of players or around someone who is blocking a passing lane. This is a kick for older, more skilled players. To see how it works, try bending a beach ball instead of your soccer ball.

● To make a banana kick with your right foot, approach the ball as you would for an instep kick. As you kick the ball, strike it to the right of center. Hitting the ball a bit to the outside

Approach ball and kick off-center.

A spinning ball will curve to the side...

... and, with prac[t] fly past the goalie[.]

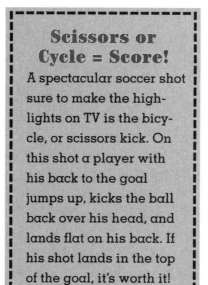

Scissors or Cycle = Score!

A spectacular soccer shot sure to make the highlights on TV is the bicycle, or scissors kick. On this shot a player with his back to the goal jumps up, kicks the ball back over his head, and lands flat on his back. If his shot lands in the top of the goal, it's worth it!

will set it spinning side-to-side. That spin will help curve the ball toward the left.

● Top players can bend a ball either way. To swing a ball the other way with your right foot, kick the ball to the left of center. Like a screwball in baseball, the reverse spin curves it in the opposite direction.

TRY IT!

How important is balance to a successful kick? Once you are making solid instep kicks, you can find out. Try to kick the ball with your hands in your pockets. Do you notice any difference?

Quick Kicker

Bryan Robson of England scored the fastest goal in World Cup history. In the 1982 finals against France, he scored 27 seconds into the game.

"The banana kick is a lot like a longer instep pass. The only difference is that you try to kick a little more to the outside of the ball."

23

PERFECT PRACTICE

INSTEP CATCH

To practice control of your kicks, try this activity with a friend. Stand about 15 feet apart with the ball at your feet. Pretend your friend is the goalie. Try to kick a ball so that she can catch it. Play close attention to the spot where your foot hits the ball. If you kick it a bit below the middle, you will get the lift you need.

When your friend makes the catch, she drops the ball at her feet. Now you're the goalie who must grab her kick. Keep working back and forth. Try instep kicks with both your right and your left foot.

Four Corners Kick

FOUR CORNERS KICK

Set up a square by placing cones, disks, or soccer balls in the four corners. Make the square about 25 steps on each side.

The three players now stand at three corners of the square. The player with the open corner on her left is player 1. He will start with the ball.

Player 1 kicks the ball along the side of the square to Player 2. As soon as he does, he runs to the open corner of the square. When Player 2 gets the ball she

turns and kicks the ball to Player 3. Player 2 then runs to the new open corner. When Player 3 kicks the ball, she will find the first player waiting for a pass. After kicking it to her, Player 3 moves to the open spot.

Start slowly so that you get the hang of the rotation. Once you do, pick up the pace. Concentrate on making accurate kicks and sprinting to the open corner.

JOG, ROLL, KICK

Start jogging forward with your soccer ball in your hands. Now roll the ball out in front of you, catch up to it, and kick it. Try to make contact while the ball is still moving. Don't worry about kicking it extra hard. Focus on getting your plant foot in the right spot and striking the ball squarely. Keep jogging, rolling, and kicking as you move around the field.

Cobi's KICKING Tips

1. On instep kicks, approach the ball from a slight angle.

2. Pay attention to your footwork. Getting your plant foot in the correct position will help you control your kick.

3. Keep your head down and watch the ball. Strike the ball at the midpoint for maximum power.

Dribbling

Sometimes when the ball comes your way in a game, your teammates will be covered or too far away to receive a pass. When that happens and you see open space in front of you, it's time to dribble.

"When you are first learning to dribble, you need to concentrate on the ball. You want to be looking at the ball, but at the same time you must pay attention to the people around you because you don't want to just go dribbling off the field or running into somebody. So try to keep your head up and keep the ball at your feet."

Dribbling during a game takes a lot of concentration. As you move the ball with your foot, you must be aware of everything going on around you. The situation on a soccer field is always changing. So dribble when you must, but always be ready to pass and shoot too.

DRIBBLING BASICS

To dribble your soccer ball, set it rolling with a series of quick, gentle taps. Be sure to keep the ball close to your feet. You can tap with the inside of your foot or with your instep.

Often a series of inside touches will cause the ball to start rolling to the side. Tap it with the outside of that same foot to straighten it out. Or tap it with your other foot to move it back in front of you.

Keep the ball close to your feet.

Use your instep or the inside of your foot.

Straighten the ball with the outside of your foot.

Dribble Tag

RATING:

A "heads-up" dribbling style is the key to this game. Mark off a small circle. Each player takes a soccer ball and dribbles in the circle, while watching everyone else. Instead of choosing one player to be IT, anyone can make a tag. A person who is tagged must stand still, but he is not out of the game. If someone else gets too close to him, the frozen person can tag her. Now she stands still as he goes back into dribbling action.

Set a time limit for this game. Play until there is only one player left, or until time runs out.

Knockout

RATING:

This popular soccer game combines dribbling with an occasional blast. The game is played like Dribble Tag, but with one big difference. Instead of tagging a player, you must try to kick his soccer ball out of the circle. When somebody's ball leaves the circle, he retrieves it and stands outside the playing area.

Games like Knockout work best when players outside the circle get a chance to return. Try adding a rule to help this along. For example, perhaps a player who dribbles around the outside of the circle can then go back inside it. Or play the game in several short rounds. After a three-minute round, players on the sidelines come back in and the game begins again.

Steal the Dribble

RATING:

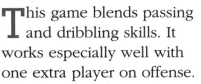

Goal Line

This game blends passing and dribbling skills. It works especially well with one extra player on offense.

Mark one goal line instead of an entire field for this game. You do not need to make a goal. Be sure there is enough room in front of the goal line for an offensive team to make its move.

As the round begins, the offensive players dribble and pass toward the goal line. They must go past the defenders and *dribble* the ball over the line. (There is no goalie or shooting in this game.) A round continues until the offense dribbles over the line or the defense steals the dribble. At that point every player on the successful side gets one point.

Now mix up the players on offense and defense and try a second time. Once again each player on the successful side gets a point. Keep mixing up the sides from round to round. Since the combos keep changing, each player should keep track of her own point total. After the last round, the person or people with the highest point totals are the winners.

LONG-DISTANCE DRIBBLES

Most dribbling is done with defenders nearby. When space opens up, you need to take as much of it as you can. The trick is to pass to yourself while you dribble quickly up field. Kick the ball harder so it rolls ahead of you. Then run and catch up to it, and kick it again.

As you become a more skilled dribbler, try to move the ball ahead with the outside of your foot. If you can learn to do this, you will be able to kick it without breaking stride. That will allow you to dribble as quickly as possible.

TRY IT!

Instead of using your soccer ball, try dribbling a much smaller target. For instance, dribble a tennis ball across the field. You will need extra focus to keep this smaller ball under control as you dribble.

"When you're dribbling, you need to think about taking the space. If there's open area in front of you, don't be afraid to push the ball into it. And you need to be sure that your teammates are following and giving you support."

Compass Corners

RATING:

EAST!

Gobbling up space with your dribbles is the key to this game. Mark out a large square field with bases at the four corners. (A base is really an area large enough so that all players can stand on it.) The bases will be called North, South, East, and West. Make sure everyone knows which is which.

One player begins the game. She stands on the side facing away from the field so she can't see where the players are. The players spread out on the field, each one dribbling a soccer ball. Suddenly the beginner person shouts "East!" At that moment every player must dribble the ball to the base as quickly as possible. When a player reaches the base, he picks up his soccer ball and stands there. The last person to arrive gets a point. She becomes the person to shout the next compass corner.

Before you start, be sure to set a time limit. Play as many rounds as possible before the clock runs out. When the last round is finished, the person with the *lowest* score is the winner.

TURNING

THE INSIDE HOOK

To make a sharp turn, lean to the side you want to go. Drop your shoulder and keep your arms out to help position your body. Your weight will be on one foot.

Tuck the inside of your other foot around the outside of the ball. Now pull the ball across so it passes right in front of you. As the ball rolls by, turn quickly and follow it, continuing to dribble as you go.

Outside Hook

Inside Hook

THE OUTSIDE HOOK

This time, reach across your body and tuck the outside of your foot around the outside of the ball. Leaning to the side you want to go, slide the ball across in front of you. Follow the rolling ball and continue dribbling in this new direction.

33

Caboose

RATING:

In this two-player game one person practices dribbling while the other one tries to stop her. The player who is the engine starts with the ball in front of her. The other player, the caboose, stands right behind her.

The engine starts moving down the track with the other player at her heels. The caboose now tries to get in front of the engine. (He should not try to take away the ball.) A clever engine will change direction suddenly so that the caboose cannot get in front of her. When the caboose finally gets in front, the engine stops. The players now switch places and the chase continues.

SHIELDING

When you are dribbling and a defender approaches, turn so your body is between your opponent and the ball. Lean into her with your arm and shoulder to keep her from getting any closer.

Shielding sounds simple, but remember that your opponent will be trying as hard as she can to get around you. So you must keep your poise under pressure. Concentrate on keeping your balance and using your strength without pushing or fouling in some other way.

As you shield, dribble with the foot that is away from your opponent. That makes it harder for her to reach around and kick the ball. Keep moving and be ready to pass to a teammate as soon as possible.

"When you are shielding the ball, you need to be strong. Stay between your opponent and the ball. You can't push him away, but if you keep your arm up it will help block him from getting to the ball."

Musical Dribbles

RATING:

A simple twist turns Musi-cal Chairs into a soccer challenge. You will need a ball for every person in the game except one. You also need a radio or some other music source.

Mark off a rectangular area with plenty of room to move around and avoid accidental collisions. Place all the balls in the center. Players form a circle around the balls.

Turn on the radio. As soon as everyone hears the music, they race into the center and get control of a soccer ball. Since there are not enough balls to go around, one person won't succeed. He must try to steal the ball away from someone else. If he does, that person must take it back or try to take away another player's ball.

Keep dribbling and shielding until the music stops. At that point the player without a ball is out of the game. Now remove one ball and start the music again. Each time the music stops, one player is elimi-nated. In the last round there will be one ball and two players. Whoever has the ball when the music finally stops is the winner.

PERFECT PRACTICE

COPYCAT CHALLENGE

Work on dribble control while seeing the action on the field. Players spread out and start dribbling. Each person controls his ball while watching all others, especially the one person who has been designated the leader. When the leader stops her ball and places her foot on top of it, all the other dribblers must do the same thing. The leader can also try other cues. She might place her hand on her head, or a finger on her chin, or her arms over her head. Or she can stop for a few seconds and then start dribbling again. See how long it takes for others to pick up each cue.

ZIGZAG DRIBBLE

To practice dribbling, set up a row of cones or plastic soda bottles about 5 to 10 feet apart. Dribble inside the first one, outside the second one, and so on down the line. Concentrate on using the inside and out-side of your feet to keep the ball close to each cone as you slip past them.

If you are playing with friends, set the cones a bit wider and try the Double Zigzag Dribble. Players form lines on opposite ends of the cone, each with a ball at his feet. Both lines of players begin dribbling around the cones from one end to the other. Now the line of players coming from the other direction is an added obstacle around which you must dribble. Be sure to dribble with your head up to avoid any crashes.

SHIELD ACTIVITY

Set up a circle with all the players standing around the edge. One player now dribbles the ball into the center. A second player enters and tries to take the ball away from her. The first player, maintaining balance and using strength, dribbles and shields for as long as possible. She keeps going until the defender gets the ball or kicks it out of the circle. (You can also set a 10-second time limit.) Then the defender gets a turn shielding while a new player enters the circle to take it away.

Cobi's DRIBBLING Tips

1. Keep your head up and the ball close to your feet when you dribble. Practice with both feet and use different parts of each foot too.

2. Try not to dribble into a crowd. If you do, keep your body between the closest player and the ball and be ready to pass to a teammate.

3. When you see an opening, don't be afraid to take the space. Dribbling into your opponent's area puts pressure on the other team.

Passing

During a soccer game, players on a team will take a few shots and score even fewer goals, but they may pass the ball dozens of times. Passing and teamwork go hand in hand.

"The first pass you need to make is with the inside of your foot. Be sure to keep the ball on the ground because that's the easiest way to make an accurate pass. After a while you can use your instep to lift the ball and make longer passes."

Many goals begin with a series of good passes among teammates. Players use a passing game to keep control of the ball as they move down the field. As the attack builds they move into position, take shots, and hopefully score goals.

THE PUSH PASS

ON YOUR MARK!

The inside-of-the-foot pass, also called the push pass, is made with the ball right in front of you. Before you kick, look quickly around the field. Find a teammate nearby who is in the clear.

GET SET!

Bring one foot forward and plant it a few inches to the side of the ball. Make sure it points in the direction you want the ball to go. As you bring back your kicking foot, turn it so your toes point to the outside. Keep your ankle stiff. Your eyes should remain focused on the ball.

PASS!

Swing your leg forward and strike the ball with the inside of your foot, just below the ankle. Try to hit the ball in the middle. As you follow through, bring your foot up just a bit. This gives the ball a forward spin that helps it roll quickly over the ground. After you have made the pass, move to an open spot in case your teammate needs to pass the ball back to you.

The Incredible Shrinking Goal

RATING:

This passing game is designed for two-player teams. Before starting, you need to make a goal that is about 10 steps wide. (For goal markers, use extra soccer balls, plastic soda bottles, or anything else that is easy to move.)

The first pair of players stands in front of and behind the goal. Each person should be about 10 feet from the goal. They pass the ball back and forth through the goal one time. Each team gets one chance. Any team that does not "score" with its passes is out.

Now move the goal markers a step closer together. The teams try to make the passes again. With

each new round make the goal a step smaller. The game continues round by round until only one team—the winning one—survives.

If there are only two of you, try changing the rules a bit. Instead of making the goal smaller, take a step away from each other after each successful kick. How many passes through the goal can you make together before one of you misses?

Circle Strike

RATING:

To succeed at this game, you must make accurate passes while moving. You need one soccer ball, a bunch of plastic cones or soda bottles, and a passing partner.

Begin by marking a circle about 20 feet across. Stand the cones or soda bottles in different parts of the circle.

Start outside the circle, with the ball at your feet and your partner across from you. Now dribble around the circle. Your partner walks around the opposite side so that you are always across from one another. Kick a push pass through the circle to her without knocking over any cones. Be sure to lead your partner so she can catch and return the ball as quickly as possible. Keep walking and

dribbling around the circle, sending passes back and forth whenever you can. Stop after one minute. Score 1 point for every pass you made, but subtract 2 points for any cones that have been knocked over.

If there are a lot of play-ers, you can form two-player teams and take turns. The team that finishes with the highest score wins. If you and a friend are playing alone, go for a personal best. After playing one time, try again and see if you can beat your score.

MORE PASSES

OUTSIDE-OF-THE-FOOT PASS

For this pass you need to change your footwork just a bit from the inside-of-the-foot pass. Place your plant foot to the side of the ball, but turn that foot so your ankle points where you want the ball to go. Now bring back your kicking foot, pointing your toes inward. As you bring your leg forward, swing it toward your teammate. Strike the middle of the ball with the outside of your foot, near your little toe.

Turn your foot at the ankle before striking the ball with the outside of your foot.

Passing Pioneers

In the early days, soccer was a dribbling game. Some people credit the Scots with perfecting the pass. According to the story, a Scottish team made the first passes in the 1800s in a match against an English team. After watching the ball zip from one player to the next, it didn't take long for other players to catch on to this radical new idea.

BACK-HEEL PASS

In some games, the team-mate who is open for a pass may be trailing behind you. If you have time, you can turn and pass the ball back. As your skill level increases, you can also use your heel to kick the ball back to him. A back-heel pass must be made quickly, especially when the ball is rolling forward.

● As you approach the ball, step over it so that your kicking foot is in front of it. Keep that foot in the air with your toes pointing up slightly. Bring your foot back and strike the ball with your heel. Remember to keep your eye on the ball as you hit it and aim your heel in the direction you want the ball to go.

TRY IT!

Can you see two things at once? You must watch the ball when you kick it, but you also need to keep your head up to see the action on the field. Place an orange cone on your head like a cone cap. (If you don't have a cone, try using a book instead.) While balancing it, try to make a simple push pass.

WALL PASS

This passing play is a lot like a "give and go" in basketball. You and a teammate use it to race past the defense.

● As you approach the defender, make sure you have the ball under control. Keep an eye on your teammate, who is moving forward some distance to the side of you. Begin by passing to her quickly, making sure the ball cannot be blocked.

● Don't stop running after you make the pass. As the defender tries to stop the ball, you move past her.

That leaves the defender out of position. Your teammate now kicks a quick return pass behind the defender. As you run forward and collect the ball, you're on your way!

"**P**ass or dribble? It depends on the situation. The simpler thing is almost always the better thing to do. If there is someone to pass to, that is usually the easier thing to do rather than trying to dribble the ball and take someone on."

Caterpillar

RATING:

This game will help you work on your back-heel pass. The more players you have, the more fun it is. First everyone lines up, one in front of the other, to form the caterpillar. Players stand with their legs apart so that there is a tunnel from the front player to the back. Choose a finish line about 20 feet in front of the caterpillar.

The player on the front of the line has the ball. He kicks a back-heel pass through the legs of his teammates to the player at the end. If the ball gets stuck along the way, a teammate can help it along, *but only if it has gone through his legs*.

When the ball reaches the last player, she dribbles to the front of the line. Now she makes a back-heel pass through everyone's legs. As players come to the front, the caterpillar slowly inches forward. Keep going until the caterpillar crosses the finish line.

S·O·C·C·E·R

RATING:

Sometimes it takes more than good aim and a strong leg to make a great pass. Like a quarterback in football, you need to deliver the ball so that it settles at the perfect spot on the field. This skill, called *touch*, is the key to this game.

Everyone uses her own soccer ball. Begin by rolling an extra target ball a short distance away—perhaps about 30 feet. Now each player kicks her soccer ball, trying to make it stop as close as possible to the target ball.

When every person has made a kick, see whose ball landed closest to the target. The person who kicked it gets the letter S. Now roll the ball away and play another round. As the game continues different players collect letters. The first person to spell S-O-C-C-E-R is the winner.

Target Ball

"**S**ome people say they are afraid of heading the ball, but if you do it the right way it really doesn't hurt. You have to focus on hitting it right at the hairline. Your forehead is really solid, and it is not going to hurt if you hit it there."

TRICKY PASSES

HEADING

Your head can be very useful when you need to pass a high-flying soccer ball.

ON YOUR MARK!

Keep your eyes on the ball as you move under it. Al-

though you are watching the ball, you must be aware of any players around you too.

GET SET!

As the ball comes down, put one leg behind the other and bend your knees slightly. Looking up, bend your upper body backward so your weight shifts to your back foot.

CHIP PASS

When a defender is blocking the path of your pass, you pop the ball in the air, or "chip" it. (This is a difficult skill that even good young players need time to master. If you are not ready to learn it, you could try chipping with a beach ball.)

● To make this pass, approach the ball like an instep kick. Plant your non-kicking foot to the side and behind the ball. As you bring your leg forward, lean back and kick under the ball. Use a short, chopping kick. Let your knee straighten, but don't follow through. If you chip correctly, the ball will pop in the air. Its backward spin will help stop the ball as it lands behind the defender and near your teammate.

HEAD!

As the ball comes down, move your head and neck up to meet it. Hit the ball before it hits you. Make sure you strike it with your forehead. Keep your eyes open and focused on the ball. They will shut automatically as you head it.

Heads Up

RATING:

Can you use your head to think and hit the ball at the same time? This game is a fun way to find out.

Players form a half-circle facing one person who has the ball. As the game begins, he tosses the ball to different players and shouts either "head" or "catch." Depending on what he says, a player hits a header or catches the ball and throws it back to him.

Play for a while so everyone gets used to heading and catching. Then change the rules, so that now when the player shouts you must do the *opposite* of what he says. You will be surprised at how much you must concentrate on his instructions in order to do the right thing.

When a player makes the wrong choice, he switches places with the person tossing the ball and the game continues. Set a time limit before you start or play until everyone has had a chance to toss the ball.

Head!

Link-Along

RATING:

This is a good game for a group of kids and a single soccer ball. Use it to practice low and accurate push passes.

One team forms a chain by standing side by side and linking arms. Each player in the chain stands with his legs apart so that a soccer ball can roll through them. The other team lines up facing them about 10 feet away.

The linked team shouts the name of one player from the other team. She must kick the ball from her spot through the legs of any player in the linked group. If she does, one player on the end of the chain breaks off and joins the shooters. If she doesn't make a successful pass, the shooter must link arms and join the chain.

In either case, another name is called and the game continues.

Set a time limit before you start. If all the players end up linked, that group wins. If everyone is freed from the links, the shooters win. If time runs out, the group with the most players wins.

VOLLEYS

A soccer volley is a kick you make before the ball hits the ground. Players use volleys to make quick, hard passes and shots. Since you only get one touch to pick the ball out of the air, this is one of the hardest kicks to learn.

STRAIGHT-ON VOLLEY

Move quickly toward the ball. Take a step forward and point your plant foot in the direction of the ball. As you do, pull back your kicking foot. Your weight will be a bit back too. Keep your arms out for balance.

● Kick the ball when it is in front of you and a few inches off the ground. Bring your foot forward and hit it with your instep. (You can also try a volley with the inside of your foot.) A short stroke works best when volleying, so punch at the ball with your foot.

SIDE VOLLEY

Use this shot to change the direction of the ball. Approach the ball and plant your foot as you would for a straight volley. Point your plant foot at the ball, but be sure your weight is on the toes and ball of that foot.

Bring your kicking leg back and out to the side.

● As you bring your leg forward to kick, pivot on your plant foot. It should now turn from the direction the ball is coming to the direction you want it to go. Bring your leg from the side to kick the ball. Again, use a quick punch of a kick with a short follow-through.

Plus Play

RATING:

This all-around game provides lots of opportunities for passing practice. When you choose up sides, make sure there are two or three people left over. These players are free to join either side as the game progresses.

The game begins like a regular soccer match with one difference. When a team has the ball, the extra players join it. They play with that offense until the other team gains control of the ball. At that moment they instantly switch sides. The extra players keep switching back and forth as the game situations change. The result is added offensive pressure on both ends of the field.

Set a time limit before you start. When time runs out, the team with the high score wins.

53

Toss Soccer

RATING:

While practicing proper throw-in technique, you can play a game of soccer with your hands. Players throw the ball to their teammates, who are allowed to use their hands to catch it. Players must also throw the ball into the goal to score.

There are some additional rules that keep this from turning into a football game. A player cannot run with the ball. If he wants to advance with it, he must drop it on the ground and dribble. At any point he can stop, pick up the ball, and use the correct throw-in form to make a pass.

Defenders can take away the ball when it is on the ground, but cannot grab it when it is in a player's hands. Although they must give him space to throw, they can cover his teammates to make that throw more difficult.

Play the game on a small field for a set amount of time. The team with the most goals at the end of the game wins.

THROW-INS

This is one of those rare times when you may use your hands in soccer. Anytime a player kicks a ball completely over the touchline, the other team throws it back into play. A player who is close to the ball when it goes out of bounds makes the throw. She stands just off the field, holding the ball directly over her head. She makes the throw-in using two hands and with both feet on the ground.

QUICK THROW-IN

A quick pass gives your team a chance to continue down the field. Hold the ball so that your thumbs point to each other.

● Lift the ball back over and behind your head. As you bring it forward, lean so that your weight shifts from your heels to the balls of your feet. Let go when your hands are in front of you.

● Follow through so that your arms point where you want the ball to go. As soon as you finish, step back onto the field. You may receive a quick return pass as play continues.

55

HEADS UP

Use this exercise to practice heading the ball. Two players stand facing each other about 15 feet apart, with one holding a soccer ball. A third player—the defender—stands between them. He faces the player without the ball.

The player with the ball tosses it over the head of the defender to the other player. She must head the ball back to him.

LONG THROW-IN

This play is useful when you want to pass the ball to a teammate farther away. Retreat a few steps out of bounds so you can get a running start. As you approach the touchline, take a long stride with your foot. It should land just before you cross the line. Lean back and bend your knees as you reach behind with the ball.

● With your feet on the ground, bring your weight forward onto your front foot. As you do, bring your hands quickly overhead and release the ball when it is in front of you. Follow through after you let go of the ball, pointing your arms in the direction you want the ball to go.

The defender stays in the middle. Although he cannot move from that spot, he can raise his hands and jump up and down to create pressure. Take turns so that each person gets a chance to head the ball.

SWITCHBACK DRILL

Practice leading a player with a push pass to a spot on the field. Set up this activity the same way as Four Corners on page 24, but use

two soccer balls instead of one. The player with the open corner to his left begins without the ball.

The player without the ball sprints to the left. The player opposite that corner kicks it to him. As the player arrives, he stops the ball and kicks it back. Then he returns to the corner where he started as the other player sends a lead pass there. As the two players send him one pass after another, the third player moves back and forth to catch them. When the running player tires, he switches places with one of the other players. She becomes the runner, and the passing practice continues.

WALL BALL

This is probably the best way to practice kicking and passing. Stand about 10 feet in front of a wall and kick a pass against it. As the ball returns, move to the spot where it is going and kick it again. Try to kick the ball with one clean touch whenever possible. Practice passing with your left and right foot. Be sure to try the inside and outside of each foot too.

Cobi's PASSING Tips

1. Practice passing with your left and right foot. You need to get in the habit of using both of them in a soccer game.

2. As your skills develop, practice one-touch passes. Quick passes give your opponents less time to react.

3. Don't be afraid of the ball. Even a header won't hurt if you learn to hit it the right way.

Trapping

S o far, everything you have learned—kicking, dribbling, and passing—begins when you have control of your soccer ball. But how do you get your foot on the ball in the first place? Catching a ball in soccer is called trapping, or collecting.

"You can try different traps from the beginning, but you want to be sure you have the basic trap down first, which is with the inside of the foot. That's the easiest way to trap the ball. You can use your thigh, chest, or head to trap, but those are harder to do. You want to focus on the foot traps first."

Most traps are made with your feet. But players at times use every part of their body from their toes right up to their head to catch the ball. The secret to all these traps is cushioning. If the ball lands near you as softly as possible you can get it under control quickly and make plays.

FOOT TRAPS

THE OUTSIDE TRAP

Imagine an outside-of-the-foot pass in reverse. Place the side of your foot just below the little toe in the path of the ball. As the ball arrives, lift your foot slightly off the ground. Pull your leg back to slow the ball.

Now move the ball in front of you and make your play.

THE INSIDE TRAP

To use the inside of your foot, point your other foot in the direction from which the ball is coming. Turn your catching foot toes out—just like you did on the inside-of-the-foot pass. As the ball strikes the inside of your foot, pull your foot back. This takes some of the bounce out of a fast-moving ball and keeps it close to your feet.

THE BOTTOM-OF-THE-FOOT TRAP

When you are starting out, this may be the surest way to stop a ball coming right at you. Turn so that both feet point toward the ball. Just as the ball arrives, lift your catching foot a few inches off the ground. Point your foot up a bit so your toes are higher than your heel. As the ball rolls under your toes, it wedges between your foot and the ground. Now step to the side quickly so that you are ready to dribble or pass.

TRY IT!

See the cushion effect your-self. Stand completely still with your muscles tense. Have someone throw a ball off your chest or leg and see how far away it bounces. Now cover your chest or leg with a pillow and have the person throw the ball again. Notice the difference?

MORE TRAPS

Foot traps are perfect for rolling or bouncing soccer balls. But if a ball is coming to you above your knee, you need to use whatever part of your body is available—except your hands and arms, of course. Whichever trap you use, remember that the goal is always the same: get the ball under control as quickly as possible.

INSTEP TRAP

This is a way to grab a fast-moving volley. With your weight on one foot and hands out for balance, lift your catching foot. Point the instep toward the arriving ball. As the ball hits the laces of your shoe, pull your leg back and down. The ball should stick to your instep for an instant and then drop to the ground.

CHEST TRAP

Stand with your legs apart and one foot in back of the other. Keep your arms out so they don't accidentally hit the ball. When the ball arrives, lean back from the waist up. As the ball hits your chest, bend your knees a bit to help cushion the ball. Step back so the ball drops in front of you.

Puff out your chest.

HEAD TRAP

Usually you will pass or shoot when you head the ball. But if you are in an open area by yourself, you can trap with it. Stand with your knees bent slightly and your arms out for balance.

Watch the ball as it strikes your forehead. At the moment it hits, flex your knees. Keep your neck muscles relaxed to soften the

Arch your back.

blow. Move your head and body back a bit so the ball drops near your feet.

THIGH TRAP

Use your thigh to catch balls that are coming just below your waist. Raise your leg, keeping the upper part pointing down and your knee bent. As the ball hits your leg, move your knee down. The ball should go down your leg and drop in front of you.

Bull's-Eye

RATING:

In this two-person game you can practice cushioning and control. In addition to your soccer ball, you need a watch with a second hand or a stopwatch.

Make a circle about four feet across and stand in the middle of it. Have your friend stand outside the circle about 10 feet away, holding a soccer ball.

Your friend tosses you the ball and you try to trap it. Use your foot when you can, but you may stop it using any part of your body—except, of course, your hands. If you trap the ball and it lands inside the circle, you get 1 point. If the ball rolls outside the circle, you get no points. In either case, kick the ball back to your partner as fast as possible. She will pick it up and throw another ball for you to trap. Play a 60-second round and see how many points you can pile up. Now switch and give your friend a turn.

As you play, the quality of the toss will have a lot to do with your success. So add your score and your friend's score together. Now play again and see if you can work together to top your combined score.

Human Target

RATING:

This trapping game gets your whole body involved. Until you get the hang of it, try playing with a beach ball instead of a soccer ball. (If you let out just a bit of air, it won't be too bouncy.) Stand about 10 feet away from a partner. As he throws the ball, you try to trap it with your body. Score one point for a foot trap, 3 for a thigh trap, 5 for a chest or body trap, and 10 for a head trap. Throw the ball back and forth. Work as a team with 10 throws each and see how high you can score together.

Long Ball Links

RATING:

In this passing game you get a lot of practice trapping in open field situations. To play this two-team game, you need a large field with a start and a finish line at opposite ends. One player from each team stands at the starting line with the ball. A second player stands at the opposite end. Their teammates spread out along spots between them.

As the game begins, the player with the ball passes it to the next player along the way. She must trap it, turn, and pass to another player. He then traps, turns, and passes it on.

Dribbling is allowed in this game, but the quickest way to move the ball will be with long kicks—so long as the player at the end of a kick can control it. Players must also judge their teammates' leg power. If you fol-low a very strong kicker, you might set up farther downfield to make the most of her kick. If not, you might come forward to trap a shorter pass.

When the ball reaches the final player, she stops it and then sends it back. Once again it moves from player to player until it returns to start. The team whose ball makes it from end to end and back again wins.

65

"**One of the easiest ways to practice trapping is to go find a wall and kick the ball off it. Every time the ball comes back to you, trap it. Remember to trap with the inside and outside of your foot.**"

PERFECT PRACTICE

CONTROL AND SHOOT

Stand about 20 feet in front of a goal, with a friend off to one side. As the challenge begins, she tosses a bouncing ball your way. You must control it and then shoot or pass it into the goal. As the next ball arrives, you control and shoot again. Your friend should try to make your job more difficult by throwing high and low bouncers.

FOOT TRAPS

This is an excellent way to practice your trapping foot-work. Two players stand about 10 feet apart. One player has a bunch of soccer balls. As the practice begins, he rolls a ball to the other player, who traps it and pushes it to the side. As soon as he touches the first ball, his partner rolls the next one. The players work together as quickly as possible. The idea is to get quick control of one ball after another.

Cobi's TRAPPING Tips

1. Watch the ball. The height and speed of the ball will usually tell you how you must trap it.

2. Always cushion the ball. Use your body like a pillow to slow the ball down when it hits you.

3. Try to control the ball just in front of your feet. In most cases that will leave you in the best position to make a play.

Juggling

Juggling a soccer ball helps you develop ball control, coordination, and balance. It is a great way to practice by yourself, or when you are playing in a small space like a backyard.

"I used to juggle non-stop. I would try to see how many I could do in a row. My friends and I used to have competitions to see who could juggle the most. We would count to see who got the highest."

A soccer juggler bounces the ball up in the air again and again without letting it touch the ground. He may use his feet, thighs, or head. If you are a first-time juggler, you might try using a balloon or a beach ball.

JUGGLE SKILLS

THE THIGH JUGGLE

Stand with your legs apart slightly and a soccer ball in your hands. Toss the ball straight up in front of you. As you release it, keep your arms out to help you stay balanced. Watch the ball very closely.

● As the ball comes down, bring up your leg to meet it. When you strike it, your thigh should be parallel to the ground. The rest of your leg bends down at the knee. Use a smooth, short motion so the ball bounces straight up in front of you.

It should go just high enough so that you can steady yourself and hit it again. As the ball comes down, pop it back up as many times as you can.

THE INSTEP JUGGLE

The basic approach is the same as the thigh juggle, but you must make the kick with the top of your foot. Since your leg will be ex-

tended when you kick, toss the ball a bit farther out in front of you.

● As you kick your foot up, point your toes and keep your ankle stiff. Concentrate on hitting the ball squarely in the center so that it does not spin away from you as it goes up. (A little backspin is all right, since it will bring the ball back toward you.)

THE HEAD JUGGLE

This time toss the ball a bit higher and step under it with your knees bent. Lean your head back so you are looking up at the ball. Keep your eyes open and watch the ball as it comes down. Moving up from your knees, hit the ball with your forehead just below the hairline.

Keep watching it so you can move under the ball and hit it again.

TRY IT!

Can you balance a soccer ball on your forehead? Tilt your head back and give it a try. Even if you cannot do it, this little exercise will help you locate the spot just below your hairline that you must use when heading a soccer ball.

"When you juggle a soccer ball, it helps you develop your touch and control. It's okay to try to juggle with a beach ball, but switch back to a soccer ball as soon as you can and stick with it."

Five-Touch

RATING:

This game helps you work on your juggling basics. The first player tosses the ball up in the air, taps it once with his thigh, and catches it. Then he tosses it and taps with his instep. Finally he tosses and taps it once off his head. As he continues to the next level, he must tap the ball twice each time to succeed. If he misses, his turn ends and the next person starts. (When the first player tries again, he continues at the point where he missed.)

Each player must tap the ball once, then twice, and on up to a set of five taps. When he succeeds, he taps back down from five to one. The first player to complete the cycle is the winner.

You can change the skill level of this game by chang-ing the number of taps. To make it easier, play up to three taps. To make it harder, challenge yourself with a 10-tap round.

"**You can also juggle back and forth, one-touch, two-touch, three-touch. You can do one-touch, and your friend sends it back one touch, then you do two-touch and you work your way up.**"

PERFECT PRACTICE

THREE-TOUCH JUGGLE

Players form a small circle, with one person holding the ball. As the activity begins, she tosses the ball up and makes three taps. (Instep, thigh, and head taps are all allowed.) On the last tap, she sends the ball to another person, who makes three taps and passes it. You can change the game by changing the number of taps each person must make.

Cobi's JUGGLING Tips

1. Watch the ball. Your eyes should never leave it while you're juggling— even if you are hitting the ball with your head.

2. No forward spin. The ball should not be turning away from you when it goes up and down. A little backspin will help you control the ball.

3. Relax and stay balanced. Hold your arms out to help keep yourself steady.

60-SECOND JUGGLE

Toss the ball up and start to juggle. You can let it bounce in between juggles or catch it in between, but count the number of juggling touches of any kind you make in a minute. Try again each day and see if you can increase your number of taps before 60 seconds are over.

Defense

Passing, dribbling, and trapping become a lot harder when you switch from practice to a real soccer game. Whenever you have the ball, someone from the other team is certain to make things as difficult as possible for you. Defenders break up passes, steal balls, get in the way, and generally make your life miserable.

"Tackling is just going in and trying to get the ball. You want to go in hard, not to hurt anyone, but hard enough to win the ball. When you go in soft or you try to pull back, that's when you get injured. So be agressive but go for the ball, not the player."

Don't get upset, though. As soon as your opponent gains control of the ball it is your job to turn to defense and do the same thing to him. Fortunately you will have plenty of help. In soccer, defense is always a team effort.

TACKLING

In football, defenders use bone-crunching tackles to stop players from moving ahead with the ball. Tackling is a big part of soccer too, though in this sport it has a different meaning. When you make a soccer tackle, you try to steal or take away the ball.

THE BLOCK TACKLE

This tackle blocks the ball so a player cannot kick it forward. Since you are in front of that player, it is

A block tackle will stop the ball, but only for an instant.

sometimes called a *front tackle*.

● Approach the ball as if you were going to kick it. As you bring your leg forward, place the inside of your tackling foot against the ball in a blocking position. Make sure you lock

your ankle. Keep in mind that the ball will only be frozen for an instant and will then be up for grabs. Immediately use your own fast footwork and try to take the ball away with a kick or a dribble.

still have a chance to set up on defense before the ball returns to the field.

THE SLIDE TACKLE

This is a last-gasp move, since you will be on the ground after you make the play. You might use a slide tackle to stop a player from getting off a clean shot at your goal. Players also use it to knock the ball out of bounds, since they can

THE POKE TACKLE

This move, also called the *side tackle*, is useful when you are chasing a player who is trying to dribble away from you. You will not steal the ball with this move; your purpose is to stop your opponent by knocking it away from her.

● Come up on the side of the player with the ball so that you are running stride for stride. Using the outside of the foot closest to her, try

to tip it away. Poke tackles work well along the sides of the field. You may not hit the ball. Even if you force your opponent to kick it out of bounds, your team will bounce up quickly and be ready for the throw-in. As with a baseball slide, make sure a coach or some other expert teaches you how to do it.

● Begin your slide when you are alongside or in front of the player with the ball. Slide with your non-tackling leg in front of the ball. As you do this, your other leg will be above it and bent. As you drop to the ground, sweep your top leg across and kick the ball away. When you finish, don't sit on the ground admiring your slide. Bounce up and get back in action.

MARKING

On defense you will often stick close to a particular player on the other team. The soccer term for this is *marking*. If you and your teammates mark all the players from the other team,

there is less chance that anyone will get loose to collect a pass, shoot, or score.

There are two basic approaches to this defense. In a man-to-man defense, you mark one player and follow him wherever he goes. In a zone system, you defend a certain part of the field, marking different players as they come into your area.

As in basketball, when you mark a player you cover him even if he doesn't have the ball. Try to keep him from receiving a pass. If he does get the ball, move forward for a tackle. If you can't make that play, try to force him away from the goal or toward your teammates. They should be ready to help you defend.

Try to force a player with the ball away from your goal.

1-2-3 Score

RATING:

This game stresses passing over goal scoring. It also creates a lot of take-away situations for players on each of two teams.

Begin by setting up a soccer field, without any goals. Choose up sides and have the players spread out. The game begins with a drop ball. As soon as one team gains control of the ball, they try to complete three passes in a row. If they succeed they score a point. The other team must intercept the ball before three passes are completed. If they do, then they try to make three passes and collect the point.

You can play the game for a certain length of time or until one team reaches 11 points. To make the game harder, require a team to make five passes in a row. To make it easier, change it to a two-pass game.

Team Tackles

RATING: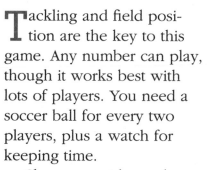

Tackling and field position are the key to this game. Any number can play, though it works best with lots of players. You need a soccer ball for every two players, plus a watch for keeping time.

Choose up sides and form two teams. All the players set up by spreading out inside a circle. Every player on the offensive team starts with a ball. The time-keeper shouts, "Go!" and the game begins. While offensive players dribble and shield, defenders try to separate them from their soccer balls. Any ball kicked beyond the circle is out of the round for good.

When a player has lost her ball, she can still help her teammates. She moves to a spot in the circle where she can receive a pass and keep another ball alive. In the end, players will be defending one ball. When that final one is tackled and kicked out of the circle, the round is over. Now switch sides and play a second round. The team that keeps a ball in play for the longer period of time wins.

OUT!

I minute!

Which Way

RATING:

This three-player game may remind you of the game Monkey in the Middle. It's a great way to work on passing and defensive positioning.

Set up the game in a small playing field. Make it a square that measures about 30 steps on each side. Two players stand facing each other just inside the square. The third player stands in the middle. He faces the player who has the ball. The player with the ball kicks a pass across to the other player. (The pass must be low to the ground. It cannot go over the middle person's head.) The middle player may slide from side to side to get the ball, but he cannot move up or back. Since he cannot see the person behind him, he is never sure where the ball is going. That gives the kicker a chance to fake him out and kick the ball past him.

When the ball makes it to the other player, the one in the middle turns to face her and the game continues from the opposite direction. If the ball is stolen, the middle player switches places with the kicker and the game goes on.

Three-Box Tackle

RATING:

This game stresses tackling, marking, and teamwork. You need about nine players on each side. When you set up this game on a rectangular field, divide the space into three equal parts, or boxes. The defenders set up with three players in each box.

Players on the offensive team line up on one goal line, each with a soccer ball at her feet. As the game begins, they try to dribble from one goal line to the other. The defenders try to tackle as many balls as they can, but they must stay in their boxes. A player is stopped when her ball is stolen, if it is kicked away from her, or if she is forced out of bounds. Since there are more offensive players in each box, some players will get through a particular box. But will they make it through all three?

The offensive team scores a point for every ball that makes it from goal line to goal line. Now the teams switch places, and the other players try to dribble from goal line to goal line. After three complete rounds the team with more points wins.

If you don't have enough players, you can scale the game down to fit your needs. For instance, with four players on a side, try playing with two boxes instead of three.

Double Soccer

RATING:

This game challenges every player to take part in both offense and defense. It sets up like a regular soccer game with one difference—each goalkeeper begins with a ball. They start the game by punting these two balls onto the field. From that moment, a team may pass, shoot, and score using either ball.

This game gives players a lot to think about. They need to be very alert to the action on the field. They must make good decisions about when to join the attack and when to drop back on defense.

When a goal is scored, the action continues with the second ball. As soon as possible the first ball is returned to the field and the action doubles up again.

Set a time limit for the game. As with soccer, high score wins.

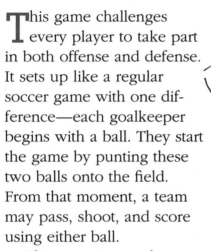

PERFECT PRACTICE

FACE-OFF

Two players can practice one-on-one takeaways. They line up with the ball at a spot exactly between them. The kicker makes a break for the ball. The instant she moves, the other player charges forward too. The defender must tackle the ball so that kicker cannot get off a clean shot. The players then switch places and repeat the activity.

MARKING EXERCISE

To work on person-to-person marking, try playing a scrimmage. Each player is assigned someone on the other team to watch who must *not* score. This forces a player to be aware of one opponent in what otherwise would be a wide-open scrimmage.

You can try this exercise two different ways. If you and a player from the opposing team are marking each other, you will travel in pairs all over the field. However, also try it so that the player you are marking is different from the one who is marking you. Now you must shift your field position and find that person every time your team loses control of the ball.

KEEP-AWAY

Two groups of players gather inside a circle. One player has a ball and shields it from a defender. Other offensive players can help by trying to get free for a pass, while defenders mark them to prevent it. Each player must make a pass or control the ball for 10 seconds without allowing her opponent to steal the ball.

Cobi's DEFENSE Tips

1. Play defense before the ball arrives. Try to prevent your opponent from getting the ball in the first place.

2. Make the player with the ball go where you want him to go. Try to guide him to spots where your teammates are waiting with support. If you are the final line of defense, guide him away from the goal.

3. Go for the steal when you see a little space between the player and the ball. Be very determined and go in strong. Commit both your mind and your body to the tackle.

Goalkeeping

Goalkeepers are in the middle of the most critical action on a soccer field. A goalie must be ready to make diving catches like a football wide receiver, and scoop up tricky bouncers like a baseball shortstop. Often surrounded by enemy players, the "keeper" makes split-second decisions about when to throw, punch, and kick the ball out of danger. A goalkeeper must be physically and mentally ready to meet every challenge. That is why a successful soccer team always has a smart, tough, courageous goalie.

"A good goalie must be an all-around player. On the Galaxy our two goalies sometimes join us when we're kicking the ball around or playing one of our warm-up games. If you want to be a goalie, remember that you need to develop your skills with your feet as well as with your hands."

THE GOALIE SCOOP

A keeper must often grab soccer balls that are heading toward his goal. When you start out, one of the most common catches involves scooping up balls rolling along the ground.

ON YOUR MARK!

Whenever a player comes toward you with the ball, take the "Ready Position." Stand with your legs apart and your knees bent. Lean forward so your weight is on the balls of your feet. Keep your hands up and your fingers spread out. (Your thumbs should point to each other so that along with your index fingers they form a "W" shape.) Watch the action on the field and be ready to move in any direction.

GET SET!

When a ball starts rolling toward the goal, move so that it will come right to you. If it is rolling slowly, come forward quickly so

Keep your eyes on the ball as you move into position to scoop it up.

that you can grab it before another player kicks it. If you must move back, backpedal quickly, watching the ball as you go.

SCOOP!

Bend from the waist as the ball arrives. With your arms down and your palms out, scoop up the ball. Keep your fingers spread out and your elbows tucked at your sides. As you grab the ball, bring it into your chest and hug it tightly. If the ball bounces away, be ready to pounce on it before a player can get her foot on it.

THE KNEELING SCOOP

Another way to catch a rolling ball is to drop down on one knee. As you get down, turn so that your knee is on the ground right behind your other foot. (Together your legs form a blocking barrier in case you miss the ball.) Turn at the waist so both arms face the ball. Scoop up the ball and hug it tightly.

Don't Blame the Goalie

Muamba Kazadi of Uganda was the first goalie ever to be pulled from a World Cup game, though not for an injury. In a 1974 match his team played the powerful West German squad and quickly fell behind 3–0. After only 18 minutes Kazadi was removed from the goal. The change in goalies did not improve his team's luck. Uganda ended up losing the game 9–0.

MORE CATCHES

LINE DRIVES

On higher shots, catch the ball with your palms open and your fingers spread out and pointing up. As you pull the ball into your chest, bring your head down. Surround the ball with your chin, arms, and body.

HIGH BALLS

When you must jump to catch a ball, leap off the foot that is closer to the spot where the ball is going. Bring your opposite knee up in front of you for balance and protection.

Zero Man

In 1990 Italy's Walter Zenga was not scored on for 517 consecutive minutes of World Cup play. His sixth game was more than an hour old before an opponent finally squeezed a shot past him.

Raise both hands with your fingers in the "W" position. As the ball hits your hands, close them on it. On a hard shot, move your arms back a bit to cushion the ball as you catch it.

DIVING STOPS

Sometimes a keeper must leave his feet, lunging to one side to make the play. As the ball arrives, dive so that your whole body stretches out, blocking some of the goal. Reach for the ball, putting one hand on top of it and one behind it. Pull the ball into your body as soon as you can.

PUNCHES

Sometimes a goalie cannot get both hands on the ball for a catch. There may be too many players nearby, or he may be unable to reach the ball and get his arms securely around it. When that happens, a goalie uses his hands to punch the ball away.

Whenever possible, use both hands to punch the ball. Clench your fists and hold them together in front of your chest. As the ball arrives, punch it as hard as you can.

TRY IT!

A soccer goal is 24 feet wide and 8 feet high. That means there is 24 × 8 feet, or 192 square feet, to cover.

● Try measuring your "wingspan"—the amount of goal you can easily cover. Try this near a wall, tree, or fence on soft ground. First jump and touch the highest point on the wall. Measure how high you can go. From a standing position now, dive to one side and then to the other. Measure that distance from end to end. Multiply the height times the width and compare your wingspan to the actual size of a goal. Can you see why goalkeeping is such a tough job?

Shoot-Out

RATING:

behind the shooting line.

The first player dribbles toward the shooting line and tries to kick his ball past the goalie. After he finishes, he retrieves his ball and dribbles to the end of the line. Meanwhile, the next kicker is already dribbling in for her shot. As soon as the goalie takes the ready position, the shooter takes her shot.

Players shoot quickly, one after another. The goalie gets one point for every shot that he stops. He then joins the shooters, and a new goalie takes his place. (If you are playing in small groups, give each shooter two or three chances before making the switch.)

Each person takes a turn in goal. Whoever collects the most points is the winner. In the case of a tie, stage an overtime round. The tied players get an extra turn in goal while everyone else tries to shoot the ball past them. The keeper who stops the most shots is the winner.

This game provides lots of shooting practice and gives everyone a chance to see what it is like to be a goalie. Play in small groups so that the action is fast-paced for everyone.

Begin by setting up a goal about 10 feet wide. Also mark a shooting line about 15 feet from the goal. (If you and your friends are strong kickers, start farther back.) As one person sets up in goal, the first kicker takes his place

GOALIE THROWS

After a goalie catches the ball she must move it forward as quickly as possible. An accurate pass can swing her team from defense to offense in a hurry.

BOWLING THROW

Often called the *underhand toss,* this is one of the best ways to make short, accurate passes to your teammates.

Tuck the ball between your palm and wrist with your fingers wrapped around it. Take a long step in the direction you want the ball to go. Take the ball back underhanded, as if you were holding a bowling ball. Now roll the ball toward your teammate. Be sure to keep your hand low to the ground as you let go of the ball so there is as little bounce as possible. Follow through with your arm pointing to the player.

BASEBALL THROW

Use this overhand toss, also called a *javelin throw,* to pass the ball a little farther. Holding the ball in your fingers, bring it back behind your ear.

With your elbow bent, step forward. As your weight shifts to your front foot, bring your arm forward and throw. If your hand is small, be careful that the ball doesn't slip out too early.

OVERARM THROW

Hold the ball between your wrist and the base of your palm. Stretch your arm to the side and back. Your palm and the ball should point up. Point your other hand and your front foot in the direction the throw will go.

Step forward, throw the ball overhand, arm straight so that it sweeps forward with the ball. As you let go, make sure that the ball goes over the heads of any opponents.

PUNT

Hold the ball in front of you with both hands about waist high. Your arms should be straight out so the ball is in front of your body. Keep your eyes on the ball.

As you step forward with your non-kicking foot, bring your other leg back. Drop the ball in front of you. Before it hits the ground, kick the ball hard with your instep. Your leg should move forward and up as you follow through. You can even hop a bit on your other foot to be sure you get all your weight into the kick.

Goalie Olympics

RATING:

This is really three games in one, and they are designed to work on your ball-clearing skills. Goalie Olympics should be played on a field with lots of space.

The Underhand Bowl is the first event. Set up some orange cones or empty plastic soda bottles in a triangle shape like the pins in a bowling alley. Place them about 25 feet to the side of the goalie. Each player gets two rolls to knock down as many pins as possible. High score wins.

The Baseball Pass is the next challenge. The players spread out in front of the goalie, who waves them into the position he wants. Then he throws the ball as far as possible to one player. Each goalie gets three chances. Players downfield must catch the throw. Whoever completes the longest throw is the winner of this event.

The Long-Range Fling is the final activity. Each goalie gets two chances, and he can punt the ball or use the overarm throw. Instead of catching the ball, let it roll to a complete stop. The player who sends the ball farthest down the field is the winner.

Back Ball

RATING:

This game is a great workout for two goalkeepers. Begin by marking a single goal in the middle of the field. Now have the keepers stand back-to-back on opposite sides of the goal. Each of them is defending his half of the field.

As the game begins, each team tries to put the ball past the opposing team's goalie. When the ball is on the wrong half of the field, players must gain control and bring it around to the other side in order to shoot and score.

You can add to the goalkeeping challenge by throwing some extra balls onto the field. With three or four balls to play, goalies will have little time to relax. When time runs out, the team that has scored the most goals wins.

94

PERFECT PRACTICE

JUMP TOSS

This is a good warm-up for goalkeepers, and it helps you work on your leaping ability and timing. Stand facing a friend about five feet away. Toss a ball up over her head. She must jump to catch it. Your friend then tosses the ball back, and you leap and grab it. Concentrate on jumping higher and higher so that your legs get a good workout.

POUNCE DRILL

Goalies must fall on any loose balls in front of their goal. Stand facing another player with your legs apart. As the other player rolls the ball through your legs, turn and fall on the ball. Now return to the starting position. This time roll the ball through the other player's legs so that she can turn and pounce on it.

BACKPEDAL EXERCISE

A goalie should never turn his back on the play. This drill will help you develop your footwork.

Stand about 30 feet in front of your goal, holding the ball. Have your friend stand 15 feet in front of you. Roll the ball to her and start backpedaling as fast as you can toward your goal. Your friend controls the ball and shoots as quickly as possible. Try to make the stop while moving back into position. After each stop, return to your original spot and try again.

Cobi's GOALIE Tips

1. Be an all-around player. Goalies must be very good at using their hands *and* their feet.

2. When the pressure is on, don't hesitate. Make the play and then get back in position.

3. When you catch the ball, hang on tight. When you punch, throw, or kick it, be sure to clear the goal area.

More Soccer

Soccer is a simple game, with few rules that get in the way of having fun. But there are some things you need to know that will help prepare you to play on an organized team.

"I think one of my greatest thrills was stepping onto the field for the 1994 World Cup. Just walking out on the field against Brazil and standing alongside great players like Romario and Bebeto. That was pretty amazing."

Tweet

THE REFEREE

From youth soccer up to the pros, the referee is responsible for controlling a soccer game. In this fast-moving, non-stop sport, he enforces many rules to make certain that a match is played cleanly and correctly. For instance, he blows his whistle to stop rough play, such as tripping or pushing. He also watches for other violations, such as a player

touching a ball with his hands. The referee decides

when teams should take throw-ins, free kicks, goal kicks, corner kicks, and penalty kicks.

The referee is also the official timekeeper. He blows his whistle to signal for halftime and for the end of the game.

FREE KICKS

When a referee signals a foul against a player, the other team is awarded a free kick. It may be a direct or indirect free kick, depending on the type of foul and the location on the field. In most cases all players must

stand at least 10 yards away from the player who is taking the kick.

A goal may be scored on a direct free kick. An indirect free kick must first touch another player before being kicked into the goal.

THE WALL

On a free kick near the goal, defenders may help their goalie by forming a wall. They stand shoulder to shoulder, blocking off a section of the goal from the kicker's view. This cuts down the open area that the goalie must cover. Of course a skilled player can chip the ball over the wall or send a banana kick around it, so the goalie must be very alert.

CORNER KICKS

When the defense kicks the ball over its own goal line, the offense gets a corner kick. The ball is placed in the corner of the field, and all defenders stand 10 yards back. The kicker sends the ball to a teammate hoping to create a chance to score.

A short corner kick is really a quick pass to a teammate. She can then dribble toward the goal, looking to pass or shoot. A long corner kick is a blast across the front of the goal. Although this area is well defended, a good crossing kick may create a chance for a quick shot or header at the goal.

OFFSIDE

As in hockey, soccer's offside rule prevents a player from hanging around the goal waiting to take an easy shot. In most cases a player cannot receive a pass on his opponent's half of the field unless there are two players between him and the goal. (That means the goalie plus one defender.) If the referee blows his whistle and rules that someone is offsides, the other team will be given an indirect free kick.

GOAL KICK

When the offensive team knocks the ball over the goal line, the defense takes a goal kick. The ball is placed on the ground in the goal area. The goalkeeper or a defensive player will take the kick. After he strikes the ball, it must clear the penalty area before another player touches it. (If it does not, the kick is taken again.) Usually the kick will go to the side or downfield to remove any chance that the other team will get an easy shot in front of the goal.

If this is the nearest defender,

then this player is offsides.

PENALTY KICKS

A penalty kick is a direct free kick inside the penalty area. It is awarded when a major foul is committed in the goal area by a defensive player. Like a penalty shot in hockey, this is a one-on-one battle between goalie and shooter. The goalkeeper stands with both feet on the goal line and may not move until the player kicks the ball. (He gets one chance to strike it.) The kick is taken from the penalty spot in the penalty area. All other players must stand outside the penalty area and 10 yards back from the penalty spot.

THE WORLD CUP

The World Cup is the Olympic Games and

Fanatical Fans

When a big soccer game is played, large numbers of people want to see it. The biggest stadium in the world is in Rio de Janeiro, Brazil, where about 200,000 people squeeze in to see a big match. The smallest crowd for a professional soccer game was 0. Because of violence at an earlier match, fans were kept away from the game between West Ham United of England and Castilla of Madrid, Spain. West Ham won 5–1.

the Super Bowl rolled into one. Every four years countries from around the globe compete for the championship of soccer. They play a tournament that ends in a winner-take-all match between two teams, with billions of people watching all over the world.

The World Cup is without question the most important sporting event on earth. As a nation's team advances through a tournament, the entire country often stops to watch the games. Businesses and even schools may close. If a game is played in a far-away country on the other side of the world, people may wake up in the middle of the night just to watch it.

In 1930 Uruguay took the first cup. The World Cup has been held every four years since then except during world wars. So far, only countries in Europe and South America have won the cup.

To date, Brazil has captured four cups—more than any other country. In three of those wins Pelé, perhaps the greatest soccer player of all time, led them. Italy and Germany have also been very successful. Each country has won the cup three times. In 1998, France won the World Cup.

PRO SOCCER

Professional soccer is an international game. There are leagues in countries all over the world. Soccer-crazy countries like Britain and Italy have several professional leagues, plus local club teams. The best players in the world may sign big contracts to play for teams in other countries.

Professional soccer is still growing in the United States. The first successful league was the North American Soccer League. Great players like Pelé of Brazil and Franz Beckenbauer of West Germany came to play in the league in 1979.

Today U.S. fans can watch the pros play Major League Soccer. Cobi Jones plays for the Los Angeles Galaxy. Many of the players have had experience playing in other parts of the world.

"My first professional experience came in England. It was right after my first World Cup. In England players approach the game as a lot of hard work. Seeing the work ethic that you need to survive at that level definitely helped me with my approach to the game.

"Later I played for Vasco da Gama in Brazil. There is more of a joy in the sport there than I had experienced anywhere before. I found myself not looking at it as work all the time, but as going out and having fun. It was also more of a dribbler's game. There is a lot of taking your man one-on-one. I felt that the style there suited my game, and I loved playing there."

SOCCER WORDS

Bicycle kick   A spectacular over-the-head kick. It is also called a *scissors kick.*

Chip   To kick the ball so it pops in the air over someone.

Corner kick   A free kick for the offense from the corner of the field, after the defense has kicked the ball over its goal line.

Cross   A pass across the field in front of the goal area.

Dribble   As in basketball, to move the ball down the field. Unlike basketball, no hands allowed.

Drop ball   Like a face-off in hockey, a ball dropped by the referee for which a player from each team battles for control.

Free kick   An uncontested kick awarded by the referee. It can be indirect (to a teammate) or direct (straight to the goal).

Fullback   A player whose chief responsibility is to prevent the other team from scoring.

Instep   The top part of the foot above the toes. The most important part of your foot for soccer kicks.

Mark   To follow an opposing player and keep track of him.

Midfielder   Also called a *halfback,* a player who patrols the center of the field, moving between offense and defense.

One touch   To move the ball with a single kick. (If you trap the ball and then kick it, that would be a two-touch play.)

Penalty area   The large rectangular space in front of the goal in which a goal-keeper may use his hands.

Plant foot   Your non-kicking foot, which is placed in position as you approach the ball.

Red card   A notice of ejection from the game issued by the referee to a player.

Shield   To position your body to block a player when you have the ball.

Striker   A special name for a central attacking forward. It is his job to create scoring opportunities and to score goals.

Sweeper   Defender who plays closest to the goalie and is the last line of defense.

Tackle   To take the ball away from the attacker. There are block, poke, and slide tackles.

Touchline   The sideline.

Trap   To "catch" the ball with your body. You usually trap with your foot, but there are thigh, chest, and even head traps.

Volley   To kick the ball before it hits the ground.

Yellow card   An official warning issued to a player by the referee. A second yellow card results in ejection.

Winger   Name for the forward who attacks from the outside of the field near the touchline.